Seen and Unseen

Or, Monologues of a Homeless Snail

Yone Noguchi

MINT EDITIONS

Seen and Unseen: Or, Monologues of a Homeless Snail was first published in 1897.

This edition published by Mint Editions 2021.

ISBN 9781513282497 | E-ISBN 9781513287515

Published by Mint Editions®

MINT EDITIONS

minteditionbooks.com

Publishing Director: Jennifer Newens
Design & Production: Rachel Lopez Metzger
Project Manager: Micaela Clark
Typesetting: Westchester Publishing Services

Contents

INTRODUCTION

I would *have you think of him as I know him, a youth of twenty years, exiled and alone,* separated from the mother, far away, abandoned by his native land and Time, *a recluse and a dreamer, in love with sadness, waiting for the time to come to do his part in recalling the ancient glory of the great poets and philosophers of his land; watching, calm-eyed and serious, the writers of this new world, to see if the old words can live in the Western civilization; and if the* sheeted memories of the Past *may be re-embodied in our English tongue.*

In the editing of these poems, I have colaborated with MR. PORTER GARNETT, *whose sympathetic assistance has lightened a responsibility, that only our regard for* YONE NOGUCHI *might authorize; and if our hints and explanations of idiom and diction have aided him and if our hands, laid reverently upon his writings, have in some places cleared a few ambiguous constructions, how generously has he repaid the debt! We gave him but the crude metal of the language and he has returned it to us, minted into golden coin. He has honored our native tongue by his writings; he has lifted the veil of convention and discovered fresh beauties and unexpected charms in our speech. And so, when I try to offer some fitting introduction to the writings of my friend, his words come back to me; his virile phrases and unworn metaphors best paint his moods. What need to introduce him, indeed?—has he not in these pages spoken for himself?*

For here in these Monologues, *he has written with absolute sincerity and simplicity, his very soul's-journal, in nocturnes set to the music of an unfamiliar tongue, in form vague as his vague moods. Though* ever unknowing of Self, *he has given to these songs the truest lyric quality;— in his* lonely cabin, even yellow-jackets-abandoned—*haunting the* midnight garden—*alone in the* dream-muffled canyon; at shadeless noon, sunful-eyed,—*in the* sober-faced evening—*wrapped in the* warm darkness *of the* invisible night—*shrouded in the* gray mystery of the mist—*under the* brave, upright rains, *or swept by the* boneless winds;— *he has revealed himself a* visitor *in this sense-world, hid in a* corner of the Universe, *delighted in his dreams and reveries, with its* shadows, *its* audible silence, *and the* poetic garments *of its clouds,—disdainful of its* Names, *its* childish play *and the* dusty manners *of the city, lonely in* Being-formed Nothing, *his soul beating against the* sadness-walled body, seeking for a casement to flit out.

So much for the journal and portrait of the man, whose shy soul roams lonelily out, picked by the incessant tear-rains, his way lost in misty doubtfulness. *So much for the subjective aspect of his visions of Nature, and his life of gentle melancholy. But of those* dreams within the Dream, *of the* "Being"-fruit *of his* "Nothing" orchard, *of his* rivulet's unknown chatter,—*how many shall understand? For his is the voice of the Occident speaking from the* iron-bodied yore-time, *where there is* place without Place, *and though he would* give the Word to the word, not less, not more than the Word itself,—*these, to many heedless ears, shall be but the unintelligible* frogs' rain-songs,—the tear-cries of the crickets on the lean, gray-haired hill. *And with his own whimsical despair, we may say,* "O Homeless Snail, for my sake, put forth thy honorable horns!"

Still it may be that some may read between the lines and find the doorless entrance *to his philosophy. With him, they may gaze through the ripples, into the* mileless bottom of the mirrory brook, *and behold his* strange shadowed world. *And seeing its mysteries, they too may wonder whether* the bird. that flies upright into the atom-eyed sky,—*or its* reflected figure that sinks down into the roomy halls *beneath the surface, is the real bird. They too may* stir the waves of reverie, awakening *thereby* some unknown motion *in that* other-world, *or with their eyes* dimmed by mist-pains, *and* fingers all bloodied by rose-thorns, *find in his* corridor of Poetry, *a refuge from the* storms of vanity-winged Hope.

Yet it were but partly true to call this symbolism. It is too vague, too subtly suggestive for that. Such moods and nuances of feeling as these are not translatable into the logical and definite processes of Occidental thought. And though on the other hand, they are not distinctively Japanese in sentiment or in art, yet one might illustrate their intangible delicacy, by one of the Ho-ku's or "inspirations" *of his own* "high qualified" BA-SHO, meaningless but wisdom-wreathed syllables,—*elusive phrases,—like* opiate vapors *changing to the changing mood.*

> *"Alas, lonesome road,*
> *Deserted by wayfarers,*
> *This autumn evening!"*

And so, who shall travel along the road where YONE NOGUCHI *fares this Autumn evening? Not many pilgrims shall find the Way, but if haply,* after the curtain of his life is drawn, *one or two, after* sailing on surgeful waves, *shall pass* this space of land,—*a* wandering, love-hunting breeze *shall welcome them—the quail's note shall jump into their* Sea of Loneliness—*and in the* ghost-raining night, *whose* shadow-mysteries *are divided by the beams of his* matchless Mistress Moon, in her chamber of unfathomable peace, *the rustling of his* willow leaves *may break into the* tuneful silence—*a sigh may* knock upon the drowsy airs, *and a voice may whisper,*—"Where is my friend?"

Well may he say, "What about my songs?" *Shall* there be no shadow,— no echoing to the end?—*or must his* Word, once uttered, ever roam about the Universe with voiceless sound! *Who, indeed, will care for his poetry?*

Ah, the ripples know! *As the* monotonous rhymed rivulet *of Time* hurries down, day by night, with her undifferent tone,—the ripples, gone down far away, far away,—they know!

Gelett Burgess
SAN FRANCISCO, DEC. 1st., 1896

Prologue

The fate-colored leaves float dumbly down unto the ground-breast,
thousands after thousands, matting the earth with yellow flakes,
Whilst the brushing of a golden, Autumn wind dreams away into
the immortal stillness.

Ah, they roam down, roam down, roam down!

Alone in the dark green shadows of the canyon-forest, I never see a
mortal behind nor before me.

Alas for my beloved predecessors passed so far away over the myriad
seas and the mountains!

Alone in the tranquillity, I see the colored thought-leaves of my soul-
trees falling down, falling down, falling down upon the stainless,
snowy cheeks of this paper.

Oh, let them sleep; let them pass, anon, into eternal drowsiness. Praise
them not, O World,—abuse them not, I pray!

In search of perennial rest, they fall down, fall down, fall down, fall
down!

Ah, they are the stuff of Eternity itself; my death-hurrying, withered
thoughts of poetry are they!

I

I COME BACK TO ME

The space of land I passed along hides stealishly away, the dusty
    manners, the dusty souls, the dusty bodies,—what the city is.
Alas, venerable Nothing! as the nothing lives out of mortal view;
Alas, worthy Death! as the Death saves the sheeted sins.
Such city, unvisible now in my spiritless eyes, might be seen as holy
    rout in unknown land.
And at last I came back to me, after sailing on surgeful waves; at this
    moment, between the Present and the Future, the Past and the
    Present,—forgetting what the world was, yestertime,—forgetting
    what I was, yestertime.
When the Future shall be the Past, "I come back to me," or "I go on to
    me," shall be as one.
What do I mean by *me*? I, whom the god made at first for me!

II

Where would I go?

Gliding downward the peace-buried, silence-toned Somewhere,
    driven by the gray Melody of the monotonous-rhymed rivulet,—
    Eternal chant of perennial spirits,
My soul wrapped in warm darkness, I lost drowsily the memory of
    times.
Roaming about the harmless sky through the chattering atoms,
    accompanied by the White Musician—the mountain breeze, more
    snowy than powdered marble—under poetry-stringed harp,
My weightless soul, round-formed, forgot the fancies of my
    shuddering passion.
But for the remembering, (nay, for the remembering even in
    forgetting) the mother,—where would I go?
Ever looking up to the high sky, heart-filled I breathe the Western airs
    under heavy tears.
My shy soul was consoled then, as if I had drunk my mother's sweet
    breath, love-frozen, out of the far West.

III

The brave upright Rains

The brave upright rains come right down like errands from iron-
    bodied yoretime, never looking back; out of the ever tranquil,
    ocean-breasted, far high heaven—yet as high but as the gum tree
    at my cabin window.
Without hesitation, they kill themselves in an instant on the earth,
    lifting their single-noted chants—O tragedy! Chants? Nay, the
    clapping sound of earth-lips.
O heavenly manna, chilly, delicate as Goddess' tears for the
    intoxicated mouth of the soil, this gossamer-veiled day!
The Universe now grows sober, gaunt, hungry, frozen-hearted,
    spiteful-souled; alone, friendless, it groans out in the flute of the
    stony-throated frog.
Resignedly, the floating mountain of tired cloud creeps into the willow
    leaves—washed hair of palace-maiden of old.
Lo, the willow leaves, mirrored in the dust-freed waters of the pond!

IV

O, matchless Mistress Moon

O boundless silence, like dense magic hair!

Poetic garments of opiate vapors!—

The mystery-guarding, forever unpublished, golden-sheeted volumes far down in the rivulet, out of Time, out of Place, under the frogs' rain-songs—

O the matchless Mistress Moon in a chamber of unfathomable peace!

These ripples of water bearing radiant lanterns (moons?) roam down;—are they not the frogs' throatful breaths?

Lo, the moon in the sea-blue sky dome! To me, a golden casement to steal through into the unknown world, tenanted by another god; where it is serene as the dreamy mists of Divinity, where it is free as frenzied clouds, where it is pleasant as wandering, love-hunting breeze.

This world is not my residence to the end!

Alas, the moon has lost her way, harassed among the leaf-fellows on the darkling hill top!

Isn't there chance for my flying out?

V

Is this World the solid Being?

Under the void-frozen vanity-spirited heaven mending cloud, this
    shadeless afternoon,—the world faced like a lean philosopher,—
The resigned poet, alone, delights in the corridor of Poetry; the god
    watches the keys of the entrance, nodding, lonely, in being-formed
    nothing.
My soul, like a chilly-winged fly, roams about the sadness-walled body,
    hunting for a casement to flit out.
Lo, suddenly, an inspired bird flies upright into the atom-eyed sky!
Alas, his reflection sinks far down into the mileless bottom of the
    mirrory rivulet!
Is this world the solid being?—or a shadowy nothing?
Is the form that flies up the real bird,? Or the figure that sinks down?

VI

Sabre-cornered Winds blow

Sabre-cornered Winds blow!
Close up thy mouth; thy thin-wreathed lips shiver under the Winds!
Already-colored words are colored more by thy gossip of another.
Thy mouth is like a keyless door for thy myriad misfortunes, in this
    floating world.
Bold words be dead! as often the word is little more than nothing.
Timid words be dead! as often the word is little less than nothing!
Give the word to the Word; not less, not more than the Word itself!
Silence is the all of Silence: Stillness is the whole of Stillness.
Behold, the Heaven above is ever dumb!—Under its Muteness, the
    Seasons change around;—the thousand trees grow up:
And lo, the never-broken curtain-canopy of heaven arches closely over
    the earth.
Alas, in this big cage of the universe, without an entrance, thy Word,
    once uttered, ever roams around the world with voiceless sound!

VII

ALONE

Alone!

Though the heaven above break down; though the earth spreads around—apart, alone, not even with my own shadow in the world of darkness; with only my withered soul, housed in the tear-rusted body,

As a motherless wind in breathless vale, as a funeral bell stealing down into the unvisible world by a dream-muffled path.

Alone with my own loneliness, with my own sadness, with my own reverie.

Alone in this ghost-raining night, my cabin walls dying like formless corpses into the darkness of vacuity.

Alone in this boundless universe, closing my mortal eyes; yet, under the radiant darkness, I am ever awake to the sheeted memory of the past.

Alas, my almost decayed soul picked by the incessant tear-rains, my one desire is to be myself as nothing.

VIII

Ah, it was Rain!

I am like a broken-hearted waning smoke out of tender love's chimney,
  changed in an instant, as a hope-decayed cloud;
Leaning upon the withered willow tree, my shy dream, as a homeless
  wind, hunts formless desire with boneless hands.
I am awakened suddenly by what?—needle-like tears of my friend?—
  alas, he may be counting somewhere his never melting tears.
Ah, it was rain!
Lo, the rivulet near by, curtains over the roomy halls far beneath.
Dead, motherless, lonely, tearful world for me!
My willow leaves wither, while my friend is gone so far away, and I
  lose his track mid frozen tears.
Alas, such gloomy clouds above, gray-haired by their sadness, storm
  about with dead-voiced sounds.

IX

To an unknown Poet

When I am lost in the deep body of the mist on the hill,
The world seems built with me as its pillar!
Am I the god upon the face of the deep, deepless deepness in the
    Beginning?

X

Alas, Nothing!

Alas, nothing!

Wisdom gives the way to untruthfulness: Hope gives the way to feeble
wisdom.

What talk, about Goodness, Badness, Success, Unsuccess, Virtue,
Vice!

Like dreams amid dreams, our lives in this floating world.

Storms of vanity-winged hope, be silent!

Alone, abroad, I lost at last my way out of sight in misty doubtfulness.

While hunting the doorless entrance of Hope, my fingers were all
bloodied by rose-thorns!

The cold-hearted sun couldn't kill my dew-tears ever shed under
spirited sorriness—ever dreaming of the ideal romance.

Alas, my own frozen dews!—formed times ago, in the mileless West,
when the sword-handed hopes swept me apart from my brother,—
far away!

XI

Dreamy Peace dwelt with me

Dreamy Peace dwelt with me, whose magic vapors enclosed me, softly
  as lovers' shadows.
I ever nod upon the graves of Silence!
I ever loll upon waves of muteness, wrapping mists about my breast.
I ever roam around the unsettled land of Dawn, where the ruins
  moulder into their rest.

XII

On the midnight Garden

My own shoes' tapping picks into my shuddering soul, which, like a wan priest in a starry heaven, floats on the unfrightening thought-seas,

In the midnight garden, taking her conscious slumber among sheeted mists issuing from the door-chink of the back hill.

Alas, the frogs' songs this night, so significant! Peace,—or War?

The leaves die into sleep, the night dews having drunk up stealishly all the fragrances of the drowsy flowers.

My Spring willow-leaves stand with their eyes dimmed by mist-pains, like swooning maidens overdrenched under rains of love.

Alas, among the willow-leaves, my bushy haired love, alone, stands with willow-boned waist, graceful as a living cloud,—dressing her silvery star.

XIII

Drankest thou snowy Dews

Drankest thou snowy dews of pleasure, write right on thy soul the taste of sadness.

Alone without friend,—abroad, I cover my ears against the wind's silly question: *"What are tears?"*
Am I a visitor in this world?—or a master of this world?
Alas, this evening of silence,—frozen darkness.
No one in my sight but a tired traveling crow, havened by our wither-faced gate.
Ah, my soul roams lonelily out, like a ghostly lantern under the rains, consoled even by the sound of the desolate funeral bell drowned by the rivulet, forgetting its way to an unknown other-world.
The icy word *alas* is made for me alone!

XIV

Sliding through the Window

Sliding through the window of sea-green Heaven,
Innocent misty vapors flit into the roomy hall of the Universe,
Exhaling from the formless chimney called Spring, out of sight, where
    the god alone, transmutes his poetry of Beauty.
The opiate vapors, in foamless waves, rock about this dreaming shore
    of April-Earth.
Alas, the mother-cow with matron eyes, utters her bitter heart,
    kidnaped of her children by the curling gossamer mist!

XV

What about my Songs?

The known-unknown-bottomed gossamer waves of the field are
  colored by the traveling shadows of the lonely, orphaned meadow
  lark:

At shadeless noon, sunful-eyed,—the crazy, one-inch butterfly
  (dethroned angel?) roams about, her embodied shadow on the
  secret-chattering grass-tops in the sabre-light.

The Universe, too, has somewhere its shadow;—but what about my
  songs?

An there be no shadow, no echoing to the end,—my broken-throated
  flute will never again be made whole!

At Night

At night the Universe grows lean, sober-faced, of intoxication,
The shadow of the half-sphere curtains down closely against my world,
    like a doorless cage, and the stillness chained by wrinkled darkness
    strains throughout the Universe to be free.
Listen, frogs in the pond, (the world is a pond itself) cry out for the
    light, for the truth!
The curtains rattle ghostlily along, bloodily biting my soul, the winds
    knocking on my cabin door with their shadowy hands.

XVII

I recall my Dream

I recall my dream, passed far away into unvisible Somewhere, out of
    Time.
Ah, I have drunk and known the taste of water this very day!
Birds (moving pleasure) sing; flowers (satisfied silence) dress
    themselves; winds (sublime frenzy) roam.
I found out, at last, my dream of last night, ever surgeful, ever excited.
Alas, I was ever heaping stones upon a baseless land!
But when will the curtain of my life be drawn down against this world
    (the world itself is ever dreaming) where I dreamed my dream?
The time should be in my hand to know.

And the rivulet hurries down, day by night, with her undifferent tone!

XVIII

Ah, my Banana Tree!

But from gossamer hall? Out from cloud-like temple? Out from mist-muffled corridor? Out from phantom-dreamed canyon? Out from romance-dead field? Out from heaven-melting ocean?—the age forgotten, naked winds roam crazily after sadness-poetry, singing their own gray songs around the world of tears.

Locking my cabin door, my humble body alone with the friendless soul (my master in this world) I cover my ears against their bloody voices.

Alas, their broken forms stand at my entrance!

Who knows!—my one-leafed banana tree may be broken, laying his corpse on the bed of icy earth.

Ah, my banana tree! who gallantly stared down this chilly-blooded world, with his one soul alone, wrapping the ghost-tenanted darkness about his soft-boned breast.

XIX

Like a Paper Lantern

Oh, *my friend, thou wilt not come back to me this night!"*
I am alone in this lonely cabin, alas, in the friendless Universe, and the
snail at my door hides stealishly his horns.
"O for my sake, put forth thy honorable horns!"
To the Eastward, to the Westward? Alas, where is Truthfulness?—
Goodness?—Light?
The world enveils me; my body itself this night enveils my soul.
Alas, my soul is like a paper lantern, its pastes wetted off under the
rainy night, in the rainy world.

XX

WHERE IS THE POET?

The inky-garmented, truth-dead Cloud—woven by dumb ghost alone in the darkness of phantasmal mountain-mouth—kidnaped the maiden Moon, silence-faced, love-mannered, mirroring her golden breast in silvery rivulets:

The Wind, her lover, gray-haired in one moment, crazes around the Universe, hunting for her dewy love-letters, strewn secretly upon the oat-carpets of the open field.

O drama! never performed, never gossiped, never rhymed! Behold—to the blind beast, ever tearless, iron-hearted, the Heaven has no mouth to interpret these tidings!

Ah, where is the man who lives out of himself?—the poet inspired often to chronicle these things?

XXI

The invisible Night

The flat-boarded earth, nailed down at night, rusting under the
    darkness:
The Universe grows smaller, palpitating against its destiny:
My chilly soul—center of the world—gives seat to audible tears—the
    songs of the cricket.
I drink the darkness of a corner of the Universe,—alas! square,
    immovable world to me, on my bed! Suggesting what?—god or
    demon?—far down, under my body.
I am as a lost wind among the countless atoms of high Heaven!
Would the invisible Night might shake off her radiant light, answering
    the knocking of my soft-formed voice!

XXII

My Poetry

My Poetry begins with the tireless songs of the cricket, on the lean
    gray haired hill, in sober-faced evening.
And the next page is Stillness—
And what then, about the next to that?
Alas, the god puts his universe-covering hand over its sheets!
"Master, take off your hand for the humble servant!"
Asked in vain:—
How long for my meditation?

XXIII

DESTINY ARRIVES

Standing by the gray-boned, naked-spirited wind, dark green through
  evening veil, the thousand leaves tremble in chilly palpitation.
Fading lips of love-dead rose sing of passed damsels' sadness (or
  pleasure?) colored, juicy cheeks.
Song-forgotten, homeless meadow lark, searching in vain the
  gossamer waves of the harmless field;—
Listen! an axe—the ghostly sound of nailing on the tear-frozen
  earth!—the chopping of wood far away,—ah, this evening!
Alas, Destiny arriving must soon be here against me!

The Garden of Truth

Untimely frosts wreathe over the garden—the staid bottom were air the sea.

Alas! from her honeyed rim, frosts steal down like love-messengers from the Lady Moon.

A light-walled corridor in Truth's palace; a humanity-guarded chapel of God, where brave divinities kneel, small as mice, against the shoreless heavens,—the midnight garden, where my naked soul roams alone, under the guidance of Silence.

The God-beloved man welcomes, respects as an honored guest, his own soul and body, in his solitude.

Lo! the roses under the night dress themselves in silence, and expect no mortal applaud,—content with that of their voiceless God.

Alone in the Canyon

The audible flakes of the snowy coldness, stirred by the silence-
　　breaker of night, the hoary-browed wind, wander down, wander
　　down the sleeping boughs unto my canyon bed.
"Good-bye my beloved family!"—I am to-night buried under the
　　sheeted coldness:
The dark weights of loneliness make me immovable!
Hark! the pine-wind blows,—blows!
Lo, the feeble, obedient leaves flee down to the ground fearing the
　　stern-lipped wind voices!
Alas, the crickets' flutes, to-night, are broken!
The homeless snail climbing up the pillow, stares upon the silvered
　　star-tears on my eyes!
The fish-like night-fogs flowering with mystery on the bare-limbed
　　branches:—
The stars above put their love-beamed fires out, one by one—
Oh, I am alone! Who knows my to-night's feeling!

XXVI

Seas of Reverie

Gossamer-surging, pleasure-foamed, dream-bodied seas of reverie,
odored with passion, waving in time without time, place without
place

My soul, heavy-weighted with the dusts of life still, alas! lingering in
the rusty, broken body, sinks downward to the bottomless bottom
of Reverie's sea, to the destiny of to-morrow, unknown at this
moment.

I hear but the words:—*"The time is at hand!"*—*"And behold it was very
good!"*

Welcome, snowy clouds, far away (frozen breath of angels?) revelling
in the poetry of their myriad changings.

I am stirring the waves of Reverie with my meaningless, but wisdom-
wreathed syllables, woven by selfless pen, and destroying these
sheets, time after time, in my mystery enveloped desire—(is not
desire but unknown action?)

Alone, dreaming as in floating poetry; my form alone in the cabin
(even yellow-jackets abandoned) under the morbid-faced summer
sky.

XXVII

I delight in the Shadow

I delight in the shadow!

The shadow seems to me as radiant Virtue, as honeyed Goodness,—as mirrory Truth,—as royal servant,—as staid Stillness,—as restful Meditation,—as watery Wisdom.

In the shadow of my own body, my Soul, eternal upon the deathless Earth, humble in the face of Destiny,—a claimless visitor, or settled master, leans upon the central pillar of body.

Ever unknowing of Will, of Self,—like an opiate vapor softly issuing from the golden rim of the moon, in the gossamer-frozen sky,— unknowing of positiveness, like the Spring breeze roaming among snowy-waisted maiden flowers.

Alone, abandoned by my native land and Time, living without lips or passion.

My Soul, silent as some dead face, contented as some idol god, seeks the hidden sheeted poetry of the Universe everwhile; and so shall seek, perhaps after my death in this visible world.

XXVIII

The Bough-Wind blows!

Ah, blows! blows! the bough-wind blows!
Don't sweep away my body and soul yet, please! I still love the world,
    whilst my dear mother lives.
Hark, the bough-wind blows, blows, blows,—dashing the dusts off
    into the bottomless Eternity!
Lo, the thousand gum-trees, waving to and fro, renovate the color of
    the hanging dome.
Autumn painting the rushing California billow-hills to a restful yellow.
Ah, blows, blows, the bough-wind blows to awake forth the spirits
    from the vanity dream!

XXIX

Am I lonesome?

My body and soul melt into the canyon solitude, which itself dreams
away into the silence-moistened space of darkness-veiled earth.

Am I lonesome?—No, not I; but our night half-sphere seems sad,
stirred in her stagnant reverie by the velvety-beamed breezes.

Let me now make the fire under the tree, and color the darkness for a
little while!

Hark! what are these voices?—Are they of the winds tapping on my
back with their phantom hands?

Alas, drowning in the airs of doubtfulness, I am surrounded by pale
ghosts!—

Let me in these moments be blind, deaf and dumb in the darkness!

I am listening to Time's footsteps that come nearer, while the lofty
moon gives me a silvern road, separating the shadow-mystery.

XXX

My lonely Soul

On the tomb-mute, memory-surging night-garden, my tear-
moistened, trembling soul creeps about, hunting in vain my love's
tiny curve lined foot-tracks, lost times ago.

The odorous, phantasmal breezes (sighs of a frozen corpse in the
earth?) blow up to scatter down over the garden the icy sadness,
that waves about the lean, faded moon, hung on a withered twig.

Drowned in the music of the unexplorable rivulet's sea-song; wet
under the endless rain tears of the crickets' cries; beaten by the
beauty-decayed sabre-shadow of tree,

Alas, my soul hides, closing its eyes,—hides in the mobile body-cabin,
praying the darkness to be a sympathetic friend!

The world-scolding night-bells of the church hasten down into
another roomy world.

Alas, what about my soul's future?

XXXI

Into the Place

I ever delight in these tender-spirited, long shadows of light-flowering
summer leaves,—lying in time without time, place without place
on the bed, my pillow resting on the sea-blue mountain-side,
formed like a damsel's waist, far away.

My vapory dream glides down with the green breeze into the mystic
land of being-fruited "Nothing"-orchard, along the silence foamed,
sober shadows of the leaves:

Alas, into the place where the two roads meet, to God Garden—to
Demon Court!

XXXII

Seas of Loneliness

Underneath the void-colored shade of the trees, my "self" passed as a drowsy cloud into Somewhere.

I see my soul floating upon the face of the deep, nay the faceless face of the deepless deep—

Ah, the Seas of Loneliness!

The mute-waving, silence-waters, ever shoreless, bottomless, heavenless, colorless, have no shadow of my passing soul.

Alas, I, without wisdom, without foolishness, without goodness, without badness,—am like god, a negative god, at least!

Is that a quail? One voice out of the back-hill jumped into the ocean of loneliness.

Alas, what sound resounds; what color returns; the bottom, the heaven, too, reappears!

There is no place of muteness! Yea, my paradise is lost in this moment!

I want not pleasure, sadness, love, hatred, success, unsuccess, beauty, ugliness—only the mighty Nothing in No More.

XXXIII

CHANGES AFTER CHANGING

The world cries out with childish tears:
The world smiles on the silly girlish cheeks:
The god forgets unbravely the death.
The universe changes after changing in countless times, from being to
    being, ever timorous, to dip the waters of perfect truth.
The sun sinks far down in the West, as a glorious king, leaving the
    never-decayed romance!—Oh, thou wilt not be up again! I want
    no silvery moon!
Death be eternal death evermore!
Alas, this ignoble changing world, the shame forgotten god,—the
    hateful world of changing!

XXXIV

Childish Play

Intoxication in delusion, dreaming in intoxication, running, forgetting, absent-minded, sadness after pleasure, loss after gain, angry-faced by unsuccess,—our lives are just like childish play.

Throw thy gold out into the trail-less mountains! Sink thy treasures down in the bottomless sea!

Thy fame is nothing; people's gossip, too, is nothing.

Applause gives way soon to depreciation. The applauder passes away, the depreciator also passes away, and the listener follows them.

Before whom art thou ashamed? By whom wouldst thou be remembered?

XXXV

The Ripples know!

Shiver-giving, lofty sounding horse's hoofs, knocking on the warm
earth, (the mouldered history of old) call to awake:—the horse's
waving mane, like heart-broken willow leaves under wanton mists,
is combed by the steel-toothed, salty winds.

The young, romance-dreaming knight, straight-bodied, singing the
lust-despising war-song, rushes along the road of chastening
adventure, his stainless scabbard inviting the moon to follow, until
finding a tired, coat less tree, its past tragedy chanted in a chorus of
sadness by the snipe-group, far away.

He leaves his horse and bending down to the water of the rivulet near
by, that reflects his hope-dead face, he asks:

"Has no Romance been kept for me here?" and comes the merciless answer,
"The ripples, gone down far away, far away, they know!"

I hear his thousand sighs as he turns his horse's head to the home road,
and I see the green face of the rivulet which, with chilly smiles,
hurries down with unknown chatter.

XXXVI

Hush,—whose Sobs?

The bare tomb stands in the wind. The veil-less moon shivers,
    breathing her yellow sighs among the naked twigs.
The broken banana leaves chant in silence, *"We are content with sadness!"*
The immovable hillside cabin is dumb, enwrapped by the thousand
    Autumn voices.
Hush! a maiden's sobs!—Are they the ripple tears of the friendless
    brook, breaking the stillness?
"Oh, my love! my love, I am here!" I murmur, but I hear no reply in the
    darkness.

XXXVII

I am a Shadow

Standing like a ghost in the smiling mysteries of the moon garden,
"Whose is this shadow, is it mine? this shadow like an ashy, leafless twig,"
    I said.
"Pardon, comrade,—away!" And my knocking voice broke the birds'
    slumber.
"Away!" I said again, *"Away from me O shadow!"*
I stepped aside wishing to be free from the shadow, wishing to be
    alone on the ever-listening night-earth. *"Oh, how long wouldst thou
    follow me?"*
Alas, death!—alas, death! O giant tree in whose shadow my body-
    shadow and soul-shadow lose themselves!
Resting now under the redwood tree, that droops its boughs to stir the
    dreamy Earth, I saw my own shadow was gone.
Leaving me to the silent monologue, *"I am a shadow, I am a shadow,
    but nothing else, my friend!"*

XXXVIII

How near to Fairyland!

White handed and yellow-veiled, the angel rocks in autumn
   drowsiness.

Listen, the dream frozen drops of the rivulet-manna melt into the
   tuneful silence!

The Springlike warmth stealing into my body, drying up the wet
   mysteries of my soul, gives me flight into the freedom of vacuity,
   into roofless unfloored reverie-hall.

Lo, such greenness, such velvety greenness, such heaven without
   heaven above!

Lo, again, such gray, such velvety gray, such earth without earth
   below!—

My soul sails through the waveless, timeless mirror seas.

Oh, how near it seems to Fairyland!

Blow, blow a gust of wind! Sweep away my soul-boat against that
   shore!

XXXIX

Ah, who says so?

Wet by the tapping sounds of rain on the roof,
My soul finding not a melodious silence—a warm reverie, stirs the
 darkness of my chamber to flight, while I lie on the midnight,
 lonely bed.
Alas! The rains nail on the roof; nay, on the darkness of the night; nay,
 on the silence of the Universe!
Being even as a lost child in the night, I hear no following tears of my
 heart-broken mother—only the rains, dripping down from the
 redwood boughs. What prattle! Is it the chatter of some unseen
 mortal?
Alas! Ought a man to be one who ever weeps?
Ah, who says so?

XL

What says the Silence?

See, the silvered leaves of the canyon moon-beams shiver, falling
  down, falling down through the redwood bough-silence!
Alas, the hundred thousand myriad leaves are scattered here and there!
  Shall I myself gather all of them?
"Who art thou? a miser of Nature?" Frightened, I look behind upon the
  stupid moon stillness of the dumb sea-heaven.
Listening to my audible emotion, I find my own body rusting with the
  antique, odorous loneliness of the night Universe.
"Where is my friend?" I knocked on the drowsy airs with my sigh. I hear
  an echo, far away,—is that the answer?
Hush! stillness again: and I lie down by the rivulet's "willy-nilly"
  chatter.
Buried to-night under the moon-leaves, I try in my blindness to read
  the heart of Nature, forgetting all of myself but the tranquillity.
"Ah, what says the Silence unto me?"

XLI

The Desert of "No More"

Until Nothing muffles over the Universe of No More, my soul lives
with the god, darkness and silence.

Ah, great Nothing!

Ah, the all-powerful Desert of No More!—where myriads of beings
sleep in their eternal death; where the god dies, my soul dies,
darkness dies, silence dies; where nothing lives, but the Nothing
that lives to the End.

Listen to the cough of Nature!

After the cough, the Universe is silent again, my soul kissing the ever
nameless idol faces of the Universe, as in a holy, heathen temple.

XLII

A Night in June

The sad, tears-wrapping cricket-songs moisten, as if by rain at
  evening, the western fire-skirt—the dying glories of the Sun.
At night, the sleeper-scorning cricket speaks, overflowing the shy,
  breathless garden, smiting my soul.
A heavy-colored darkness swallows up the blushing-cheeked,
  shuddering roses.

I hear but the soundless voices; *"the Sun should be displaying his
  to-morrow's splendors."*
Alas, the Universe has no death, but only changing.
At the approach of dawn, the broken-throated, shame-pronouncing
  cricket-flutes stop their syllables against the mirrory-breasted
  rising Sun.
Yea, the things unvisible or visible change ever to the end!

XLIII

Eternal Death

My soul floats with furled desires to the place wheresoe'er I will, with printless steps, drowsily, musically, opening its eye-lashes, veiling its cheek-smiles like a thief,—

Like wanton winds, wing-disturbed, like a bushy-haired cloud with long and dusty beard.

The eternal death is a triumph to me; my beamless soul, like a twilight-mist, floats upon unchanging, uncolored, tasteless, soundless, serene seas of roofless, floorless darkness.

There I hoe the poetry-planted garden of silence; there I plow the pearl-fruited orchard of meditation.

I sing the song of my heart strings, alone in the eternal muteness, in the face of God.

XLIV

Differences

The beginning, the end—the birth, the death—the darkness, the
    light,—the voice, the silence,—the prosperity, the decay,—the love,
    the envy,—the pleasure, the suffering,—the awakening, the
    sleeping,—these differences, coming in unconscious mood, are
    what I ever welcome.
My soul-casement being opened full widely for the jealous god, who
    lives proudly under the same roof with the true god.
The juiceless flower-cheeks and the withered-green tree-hairs invite
    ever my soul, in this dusty world, to count the drops of smile-
    frozen tears and tear-frozen smiles.

XLV

The Shadow of the Trees

In this moment the flute-silent birds forget their fancies and fly up
    the high heaven, chroniclers to the shy goddess, leaving to me the
    whole of the dumb Universe, muffled in a gossamer reverie.

The noon-cloud, that disturbs the heart of the sadness-welcoming
    mortal, passes far away into an unknown shadow—ah, what is the
    fate of that cloud?—wishing to leave me contented, alone in the
    solitude.

Separated from the world-trouble, I rest under the shadow of the trees,
    until my soul-lake dustless, radiant-rippled, seems like a silvery
    mirror for a serene beauty;

And I look up the doom-visible vault of heaven, moulding my face
    into the unfathomable poetry of the sea-blue sky.

XLVI

Hiding in the Mist

In rustic loneliness, the hill-side cabin stands enwrapped by the gray
   mystery—the dream-mists.
Alas, my cabin-boat, without oars on the nightmare billow-mists,
   knows no shore whereon to anchor; floating on, she longs for the
   kindness of a blast of wind!
Alas, such abandoned cabin on the earth!
Alas, such friendless soul of me!
How long should I be hiding in the silence?
"Listen! What says my little bough-dew?"
I open the door of my cabin, and the silver-breasted rivulet-maiden,
   crawling into the mist, cries out her tears.
"Ah, what says she, my little dew on the roof?"
Alone in the cabin,—in the mystery,—in the silence, I have not
   known for a long time a mother's message.
"Ah what says she, my little dew on the window?"
Alas, who can say the heaven-pillars are not broken off this day? Who
   can say the earth-floor has not fallen down?

XLVII

The Night-Lyre echoes

Resting on my pillow, the strings of the night-lyre echo in my ears,
the storm reveling in the wall-less chamber of heaven, under the
dim lanterns of the stars.

Alas, the lantern-fires, burning up my forgotten love-sheets, bid the
mist-wreathed phantoms laugh me to scorn.

Enclosed by stillness, ghosts live there alone. What welcome fate,
then, for me!

Even my friend the broken-hearted banana tree at my cabin door
sleeps like a strange idol.

"O storm, for my sake, make my friend chant his sadness again, again!"

O smileless silence of midnight!—Now the barking of a dog, far away,
ripples lonelily along the waves of tears.

The untimely chatter of a flying meadow lark drops away into the
unknown West.

Ah, what about my own sweet love!

XLVIII

The Summer's lean Face

O ripple-creamed, high-born moon-sickle, like some angel's proud
   eye-brow, clipped off by a rushing sabre-blast!
O dead ghost's garments of darkness,—the tangled-haired sheets of
   cloud!
The fluting of the crickets' shuddering tear-songs wave over the garden.
Fearing one shiver might break their frail flutes, my lonely, boatless
   soul, still as a frozen stone, drowns in the bottom of the sea of air.
The drowsy breeze, out of the western, dying fire, drifting along the
   trail between the earth-bones, knocking the leafy door with gloved
   hands, finds a resting place in the acacia trees.
How fair the lean face of summer-evening-earth; but alas, what
   suffocating scene, as of some sick-chamber!

YONE NOGUCHI

XLIX

I am what I like to be

Art *thou plundered, my half-a-day?*" I have lost just half a day!
I closed up my mouth; the time had no power to control over me,
    separated from the whole world.
I knelt down as a humble servant before my soul,—forgetting my life,
    my fancy, my knowledge, my wisdom, my thought.
Alone in my cabin, I closed down the casement of my eyes,—I walled
    up the entrance of my ears, and the odors of the world visited in
    vain my nostrils.
Sadness, gladness, question, answer, coming breath, departing breath,
    this day left my soul!
I am what I like to be; Spring, Autumn, poverty, friends, the world
    and myself all are dead to me!
But for civility, my door would never be opened to the floating world!

My Universe

We roam out,—
Selfless, will-less, virtueless, viceless, passionless, thoughtless, as
drunken in Dreamland of Dawn, or of Nothing, into visible
darkness—this world that seems like Being.
We go back again,—
Contentless; despairless,—a thing but of Nothing:
Into this unvisible world, or visible, nothing-formed world, as storm-
winged winds die stealishly away, in the open spiritless face of the
field.
What about Goodness?
Like the winds above, formless-formed, driving mystery-iced clouds
into a mountain-mouth.
What about Wisdom?
Like winds, matron-faced, scattering flower seeds around an
unexpecting land.
The world is round; no-headed, no-footed, having no left side, no
right side!
And to say *Goodness* is to say *Badness*:
And to say *Badness* is to say *Goodness*.
The world is so filled with names; often the necessity is forgotten,
often the difference is unnamed!
The Name is nothing!
East is West,
West is East:
South is North,
North is South:
The greatest robber seems like saint:
The cunning man seems like nothing-wanted beast!
Who is the real man in the face of God?
One who has fame not known,
One who has Wisdom not applauded,
One who has Goodness not respected:
One who hasn't loved Wisdom dearly,

One who hasn't hated Foolishness strongly!

The good man stands in the world like an unknown god in
Somewhere; where Goodness, Badness, Wisdom, Foolishness
meet face to face at the divisionless border between them.

A Note About the Author

Yone Noguchi (1875–1947) was a Japanese poet, novelist, and critic who wrote in both English and Japanese. Born in Tsushima, he studied the works of Thomas Carlyle and Herbert Spencer at Keio University in Tokyo, where he also practiced Zen and wrote haiku. In 1893, he moved to San Francisco and began working at a newspaper established by Japanese exiles. Under the tutelage of Joaquin Miller, an Oakland-based writer and outdoorsman, Noguchi came into his own as a poet. He published two collections in 1897 before moving to New York via Chicago. In 1901, he published *The American Diary of a Japanese Girl*, his debut novel. Noguchi soon tired of America, however, and sailed to England where he published a third book of poems and made connections with such writers as William Butler Yeats and Thomas Hardy. Reinvigorated and determined to continue his career, he returned to New York in 1903, but left for Japan the following year following the end of his marriage to journalist and educator Léonie Gilmour, with whom he had a son. As the Russo-Japanese War brought his nation onto the world stage, Noguchi became known as a literary critic for the *Japan Times* and focused on advising such Western playwrights as Yeats to study the classical Noh drama. He spent the second decade of the century as a prominent international lecturer, mainly in Europe and Britain. In 1920, Noguchi published *Japanese Hokkus*, a collection of short poems, before turning his attention to Japanese-language verse. As Japan moved closer toward war with the West, Noguchi turned from leftist politics to the nationalism supported by his country's leaders, straining his relationship with Bengali poet Rabindranath Tagore and distancing himself from his former colleagues around the world. In 1945, his home in Tokyo was destroyed in the devastating American firebombing of the city; he died only two years later, having reconnected with his son Isamu.

A Note from the Publisher

Spanning many genres, from non-fiction essays to literature classics to children's books and lyric poetry, Mint Edition books showcase the master works of our time in a modern new package. The text is freshly typeset, is clean and easy to read, and features a new note about the author in each volume. Many books also include exclusive new introductory material. Every book boasts a striking new cover, which makes it as appropriate for collecting as it is for gift giving. Mint Edition books are only printed when a reader orders them, so natural resources are not wasted. We're proud that our books are never manufactured in excess and exist only in the exact quantity they need to be read and enjoyed.

bookfinity™

Discover more of your favorite classics with Bookfinity™.

- Track your reading with custom book lists.
- Get great book recommendations for your personalized Reader Type.
- Add reviews for your favorite books.
- AND MUCH MORE!

Visit **bookfinity.com** and take the fun Reader Type quiz to get started.

Enjoy our classic and modern companion pairings!

Classic & Modern